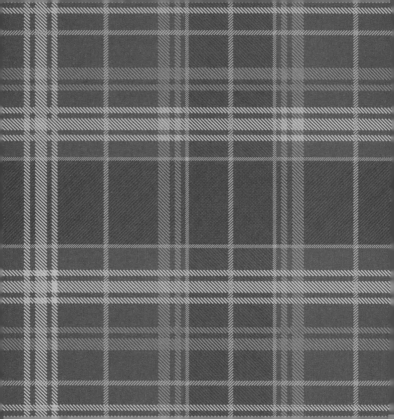

You Know You're
Past It
When...

START

Ben Fraser

summersdale

YOU KNOW YOU'RE PAST IT WHEN...

Summersdale Publishers Ltd
46 West Street
Chichester
West Sussex
PO19 1RP
UK

www.summersdale.com

Printed and bound in China

ISBN: 978-1-84953-071-2

Substantial discounts on bulk quantities of Summersdale books are available to corporations, professional associations and other organisations. For details contact Summersdale Publishers by telephone: +44 (0) 1243 771107, fax: +44 (0) 1243 786300 or email: nicky@summersdale.com.

To..

From..

That twinkle in your eye is only the sun reflecting off your bifocals.

You finally realise the virtues of
wearing socks with sandals.

You always have your mobile phone switched off because you don't want the batteries to run down, so no one can get hold of you in emergencies.

You no longer have bad hair days – you have bad hair years.

1967

1977

1987

You have a wardrobe full of clothes
that you're hoping will come back into
fashion... and they have – twice.

You think an ASBO is a brand
of deodorant.

Your partner is half your age
and it's totally legal.

It takes you twice as long to look
half as good.

Your idea of happy hour is sitting
down with a cup of tea and this week's
sudoku puzzle.

You think Dizzee Rascal is a kids' TV character.

You still carry ten pence to make an emergency call from a phone box.

You finally resist the urge
to diet.

Your waist size is measured in feet
rather than inches.

After one sip of sherry,
you're anyone's.

You can no longer control the irresistible urge to tut at anything that annoys you.

You've still got it – but nobody wants to see it.

You're not against Facebook – you just don't have the foggiest what it is.

Your back goes out more than
you do.

You can no longer distinguish between teenage boys and girls, especially as they now all seem to have long hair and wear mascara.

You think *Heat* magazine is the Fire Service's in-house newsletter.

Your partner no longer buys you sexy
lingerie for Valentine's Day, but slippers
and a hot water bottle.

You pull a muscle playing
air guitar.

Your sideburns are 7 inches long and combed over the top of your head.

Just For Men no longer refers to your
weekly poker night, but to
your shampoo.

You refer proudly to your O levels and no one understands you.

Those notches on your bedpost are a sign of woodworm infestation rather than sexual prowess!

You realise they're playing
your favourite song on
Saga FM.

You go to a party and find you're
wearing the same dress as your
friend's mother.

Your spouse nominates you to go on the nation's favourite makeover TV show.

Your car has a tape deck.

You are the star contributor to
the Status Quo fanzine.

Beautiful young women now only think
of you as their best friend's father.

Sleeping on a sofa is simply out of the question – unless you have a particularly attractive chiropractor.

Your fridge is no longer simply
somewhere to store wine and ice.

Your frequent trips to the pharmacy are for indigestion tablets and painkillers – rather than condoms and pregnancy tests.

Your idea of going out on a Saturday night is late-night shopping at the supermarket.

The health of elderly
neighbours begins creeping
into general conversation.

You take up crochet and create effigies of your favourite TV soap characters.

You wear rather more than a smile in bed these days – thermal long johns, two vests, bed socks and an electric blanket to top it off.

Six a.m. is newspaper-in-bed time, not taxi-home time.

Your main priorities while shopping for clothes are comfort and durability – and good style never goes out of fashion, right? (Er...)

Your waistband is halfway up
your chest.

Your karaoke song of choice is 'Puppy Love', which you dedicate to your first love, Donny.

After carrying your nephew up to bed,
it's you that needs to have a nap.

You've succumbed to the temptation to
wear corduroy – next step:
elbow patches.

Getting some action means the prune juice is finally kicking in.

You no longer try to ride the shopping
trolley down the aisle at
the supermarket.

You can remember smoking – inside.

You still believe the beehive is the height of fashion.

Your teen pin-ups were Rita Hayworth, Betty Grable and Ingrid Bergman.

You carry a plastic bag in your pocket
at all times in case you need to stop
and have a sit down when out
for a walk.

You give up all your bad habits
but you still don't feel or look
any better for it.

Just as your car insurance premium finally goes down, the cost of your life insurance goes up.

Your idea of getting high is consuming
three espressos back to back.

It's your doctor giving you a caution to slow down, not the police.

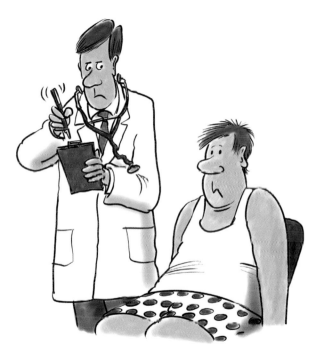

You finish all your text messages with 'Yours sincerely'.

You can't give a box of chocolates without saying, 'All because the lady loves Milk Tray' and then jumping out the window.

Your friends begin buying you
anti-wrinkle cream for
your birthday.

You prefer to buy the DVD of your favourite rock band rather than see them live.

You go on holiday and run out of
energy before running out of money.

All your friends are on Twitter but you can't work out why they're not interested in coming round to view your new bird bath.

BIRDBATH
VIEWING
TODAY

You still love to have sex on the beach
– unfortunately now it's only a cocktail.

You know who shot J. R.

You begin to agree with your dad's political views.

You think the Twist is still the dance all the kids are doing these days.

85

Having a 'quickie' means grabbing a
sneaky forty winks on the bus
ride home.

You read this whole book hoping to find one thing that didn't apply to you.

Have you enjoyed this book?
If so, why not write a review
on your favourite website?

Thanks very much for buying
this Summersdale book.

www.summersdale.com

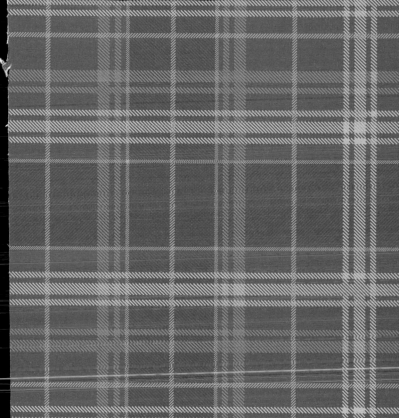